Reproducible Resource

Bullying

> Identify

> Cope

> Prevent

Grades 3 – 4

D1501746

World Teachers Press®

www.worldteacherspress.com

Published with the permission of R.I.C. Publications Pty. Ltd.

First published by R.I.C. Publications Pty. Ltd., Perth, Western Australia. Revised by Didax Educational Resources.

Printed in the United States of America.

Order Number 2-5214
ISBN 1-58324-156-6

D E F G H 10 09 08 07 06

395 Main Street
Rowley, MA 01969
www.didax.com

Foreword

Bullying has been likened by some commentators to lifestyle physical ailments prevalent in modern society, such as obesity, smoking-related disease, heart disease and even skin cancers. The "likeness" is that, in a majority of cases, adequate and appropriate preventive measures will stop the condition from arising altogether. All too often, bullying is treated as a condition only after it manifests itself, rather than pre-emptively, before it actually arises.

Bullying is a complex issue. It requires an ongoing education of students to develop skills and strategies to allow them to IDENTIFY, COPE with and, ultimately, PREVENT bullying from occurring.

This series provides developmental activities to promote positive attitudes in students, forestalling the development of injurious, bullying behavior.

Titles in this series:
Bullying, Grades 3–4
Bullying, Grades 5–6
Bullying, Grades 7–8

Contents

Teacher's Notes

Each student page is supported by a teacher's page which provides the following information.

Specific **indicators** explain what the students are expected to demonstrate through completing the activities.

Teacher information provides the teacher with detailed additional information to supplement the student page.

Did You Know? is a collection of background information on bullying behavior, covering interesting statistics and informative research facts.

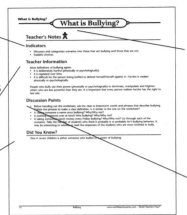

The icons below indicate the focus of each activity. Some activities may have more than one icon.

 Activities to assist students to **identify** bullying behavior and why people bully.

 Activities to help students **cope** with bullying behavior.

 Activities where students learn strategies to **prevent** bullying behavior in themselves and/or others.

Discussion Points have been suggested to further develop ideas on the student page.

Each book is divided into four sections.

What Is Bullying? (pages 14 – 33)

The activities in this section give students opportunities to identify what bullying is and the various forms it can take.

Most definitions of bullying agree:
- It is deliberately hurtful, either physically or psychologically.
- It is repeated often over time.
- It is difficult for the person being bullied to defend himself/herself against it – he/she is weaker physically or psychologically.

Bullying can be divided into three types:
1. Physical – including hitting, punching, shoving, pinching, tripping, spitting, scratching, damaging, hiding or stealing belongings, throwing objects at someone, or locking someone in or out
2. Verbal – name-calling, making offensive remarks, taunting, teasing, put-downs
3. Emotional – spreading rumors, gossiping about or embarrassing someone, making fun of someone, using threatening looks or gestures, excluding or threatening to exclude from groups, ignoring, ostracizing or alienating

Note: In each level of *Bullying*, the word "bully" is used as a verb and not a noun. In this way, the bullying behavior is emphasized and not the child. Instead of labeling a child a "bully," he/she is referred to as "a person who bullies."

Why Do People Bully? (pages 34 – 43)

People bully for a wide variety of reasons. These include feeling they don't fit in, disliking themselves, peer pressure, wanting to show off, feeling upset or angry, or having a fear of being bullied themselves. This is not necessarily due to low self-esteem or insecurity; in fact, it can be quite the opposite. However, most people who bully have a lack of empathy, which can be caused by poor parenting, a lack of good role models or be a personality trait that needs fostering in a positive direction.

In this section, students are encouraged to explore and discuss bullying scenarios and consider possible reasons for each. Teachers will also find useful activities to help them work on anger management with students. In addition, students will learn that those who bully vary widely in physical appearance and background.

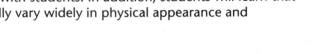

Teacher's Notes

How Does Bullying Make You Feel? (pages 44 – 51)

The activities in this section emphasize the importance of respecting the feelings and emotions of others. They require students to "put themselves in the shoes" of the person being bullied and the person who is bullying. Students are encouraged to empathize with others and to understand and deal with their own feelings. The peer group which support and reinforce the bullying behavior is also encouraged to develop empathy for the person being bullied.

The advantages of using this approach include:
- Everyone gains a clear understanding of what bullying is.
- The focus is on finding a solution and not finding someone to blame.
- The person being bullied is able to express his or her feelings and deal with the situation.
- When people around develop empathy for the person being bullied, the dynamics of the situation change.
- Many instances of bullying rely on keeping information quiet.
  However, where the feelings on bullying are known to everybody it is harder for the bullying practices to continue.
- Understanding the feelings of all involved can help lay the foundations for proactive prevention of potential bullying situations.

It is recommended that a set of rules on speaking and listening be established in the classroom, with students given the chance to regularly discuss a variety of subjects so an environment exists where they feel safe to express their feelings. If such a safe environment exists, the discussion sections accompanying each activity should produce better results and maximum participation.

What Can You Do? (pages 52 – 71)

This section of the book provides different strategies to help students cope with and prevent bullying behavior. It offers activities that promote a school ethos where bullying is openly discussed and seen as unacceptable behavior. Students are given the opportunity to discuss tolerance and friendship and to learn strategies to promote communication, problem solving and conflict resolution. Those students who are assertive and can discuss their feelings will develop a higher self-esteem and are less likely to become victims or people who bully.

Teaching problem-solving strategies through discussion and role-playing will assist students to learn and develop skills for positive social behaviors and relationships. Beginning sentences with "I" statements, having confident body language and being assertive without becoming aggressive, can be very effective ways of letting someone who is showing bullying behavior know that his/her actions will not be tolerated. Teachers can help by running drama sessions where students participate in exercises where they need to stand confidently, use eye contact and speak clearly. Deep breathing to relax the body can also help.

Students can be taught to use other strategies to deal with bullying behavior, such as avoiding the situation whenever possible and knowing when to ask for help. Asking for help is essential, especially for victims who are not able to attempt the strategies above or for those who have tried these techniques and find they are not working. Some bullying situations can be stopped early on before the bullying cycle begins through intervention by peers, teachers, parents, or other adults.

Teacher's Notes

Working with Parents

Support from parents is vitally important to help encourage a "non-bullying" environment in the classroom or school. Parental approval is very important to students and most parents are eager to support anti-bullying programs. Parents are also often the first to detect signs that their child is being bullied or is bullying others.

Teachers can encourage parents to become involved by:
- encouraging open communication
- providing bullying information and statistics
- encouraging them to watch for signs that their child is involved in a bullying situation, and to report it as soon as possible
- taking parents' concerns about bullying seriously
- asking them to discourage their child from using bullying behavior
- giving advice on how to solve conflict without violence or aggression
- encouraging them to talk to their child about what is happening at school

Tips for Creating a Non-bullying School Environment

Much has been documented and written on the subject of bullying and findings between schools may differ. However, the approach universally agreed on is that for schools to successfully and effectively tackle the problem of bullying, a whole-school approach is needed.

Successful anti-bullying initiatives have included the following:
- Include teachers, students, administration staff, parents and even the wider community in the consultation process, and the development and implementation of policy.
- Collect information about bullying in your school and define a whole-school philosophy.
- Create a written policy document that presents a mission statement, the rights and responsibilities of students, teachers and parents, and the procedures.
- Make the policy well known.
- Ensure active supervision on the school grounds and help create situations that teach students how to play and interact together.
- Acknowledge the important role that bystanders can play in reducing bullying.
- Teach non-aggressive strategies such as problem-solving and conflict-resolution skills.
- Continually monitor and maintain the policy.
- Create team-based social relationships at the class level and encourage participation by all students. Provide opportunities for all students to get to know each other well.
- Measure social relationships between students at a class-level and be aware of potential bullying problems.
- Be aware of early warning signs.

Teacher's Notes

Explanations of the generic pages included in this book are outlined below.

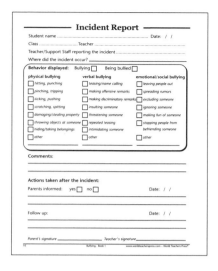

I Have a Problem (page 8) is constructed for students who have experienced bullying behavior. The students describe the problem in pictures or words and color the strategies they will use if they are in a similar situation again.

I Have Been Hurting Other People (page 9) is designed to be completed by students who have instigated or participated in bullying behavior. The student describes the incident in pictures or words and considers ways he or she can solve the problem.

The *Incident Report* (page 10) can be used by teachers and support staff to record bullying incidents. The teacher can detail any procedures introduced as a result of the event and keep records of parental involvement and follow-up actions.

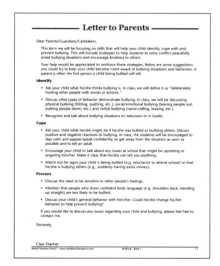

A *Letter to Parents* (page 11) is provided to inform and gain the support of parents and caregivers concerning bullying behavior.

Merit Certificates (page 12) are included to recognize and promote positive behavior.

I Have a Problem

Name: .... Class:........................ Date: / /

Draw what happened.

Write what happened. _____

_____

_____

What did you do? _____

_____

If this happens again – what would be the best thing(s) to do?

Has this ever
happened to
you before?

(Yes) (No)

| Ask the bully to STOP! | Go to a safe place. | Tell a teacher. | Play with someone else. |

Student's signature _____

Teacher's signature _____

I Have Been Hurting Other People

Name: .... Class:....................... Date: / /

Draw what happened.

Write what happened. _____

_____

What could you do to solve the problem ?

• I could listen to what the other person has to say. ☐

• I could say sorry if I hurt the other person's feelings. ☐

• I could talk with the other person about a way to solve this problem. ☐

• I could shake hands with the other person. ☐

> What are you going to do to help the person you hurt feel safe and happy?

_____

_____

_____

_____

Student's signature _____   Teacher's signature _____

Incident Report

Student name: .... Date: / /

Class: ....Teacher: ....

Teacher/Support Staff reporting the incident: ....

Where did the incident occur? _____

Behavior displayed: Bullying ☐ Being bullied ☐

physical bullying	verbal bullying	emotional/social bullying
☐ hitting, punching	☐ teasing/name calling	☐ leaving people out
☐ pinching, tripping	☐ making offensive remarks	☐ spreading rumors
☐ kicking, pushing	☐ making discriminatory remarks	☐ excluding someone
☐ scratching, spitting	☐ insulting someone	☐ ignoring someone
☐ damaging/stealing property	☐ threatening someone	☐ making fun of someone
☐ throwing objects at someone	☐ repeated teasing	☐ stopping people from befriending someone
☐ hiding/taking belongings	☐ intimidating someone	
☐ other	☐ other	☐ other

_____   _____   _____

Comments:

_____

_____

Actions taken after the incident:

Parents informed: yes ☐   no ☐   Date: / /

_____

_____

Follow up: Date: / /

_____

_____

Parent's signature _____ *Teacher's signature* _____

Letter to Parents

Dear Parents/Guardians/Caretakers,

This term we will be focusing on skills that will help your child identify, cope with and prevent bullying. This will include strategies to help students to solve conflict peacefully, avoid bullying situations and encourage kindness to others.

Your help would be appreciated to reinforce these strategies. Below are some suggestions you could try to help your child become more aware of bullying situations and behaviors. A parent is often the first person a child being bullied will tell.

Identify

- Ask your child what he/she thinks bullying is. In class, we will define it as "deliberately hurting other people with words or actions."

- Discuss what types of behavior demonstrate bullying. In class, we will be discussing physical bullying (hitting, pushing, etc.), social/emotional bullying (leaving people out, putting people down, etc.) and verbal bullying (name-calling, teasing, etc.).

- Recognize and talk about bullying situations on television or in books.

Cope

- Ask your child what he/she might do if he/she was bullied or bullying others. Discuss positive and negative reactions to bullying. In class, the students will be encouraged to stay calm and act and speak confidently, to get away from the situation as soon as possible and to tell an adult.

- Encourage your child to talk about any issues at school that might be upsetting or angering him/her. Make it clear that he/she can tell you anything.

- Watch out for signs your child is being bullied (e.g. reluctance to attend school) or that he/she is bullying others (e.g., suddenly having extra money).

Prevent

- Discuss the need to be sensitive to other people's feelings.

- Mention that people who show confident body language (e.g. shoulders back, standing up straight) are less likely to be bullied.

- Discuss your child's general behavior with him/her. Could he/she change his/her behavior to help prevent bullying?

If you would like to discuss any issues regarding your child and bullying, please feel free to contact me.

Sincerely,

Class Teacher

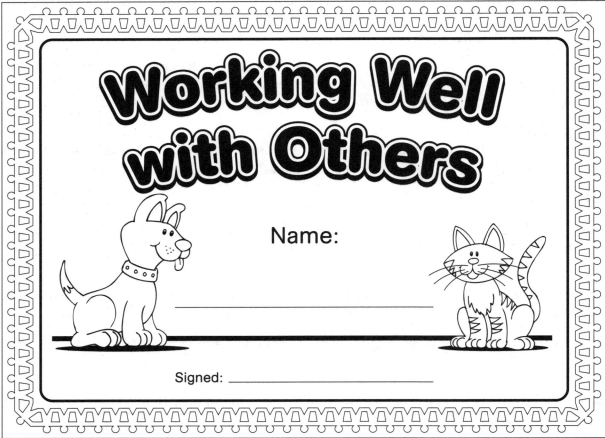

Working Well with Others

Name:

_____

Signed: _____

I'm a Great Friend

Name:

_____

Signed: _____

I Did It!

Well Done for:

_____

Signed: _____

The Three Little Pigs

Teacher's Notes

Indicator

Identifies bullying behavior of a character in a fairy tale.

Teacher Information

Identifying bullying behavior of characters in fairy tales can be used to introduce the topic to younger students. Students can observe and discuss make-believe characters bullying or being bullied before real-life situations are discussed.

In fairy tales, the conflict is usually solved and everyone lives happily ever after. These outcomes are not always appropriate to real life. For example, the wolf, who was bullying, ended up in a pot of boiling water! Concentrate on the bullying behavior in the stories instead!

Other suitable fairy tales are:
• The Three Billy Goats Gruff (where the troll is bullying)
• Cinderella (where the stepmother and two ugly stepsisters are bullying)
• The Ugly Duckling (the young swan is being bullied by the ducks)

Discussion Points

The Three Little Pigs and other fairy tales can be used to present examples of bullying behavior. In whatever fairy tale is used, focus on these points:
1. Which character(s) is/are doing the bullying?
2. Which character(s) is/are being bullied?
3. List the ways the character(s) is/are being bullied.
4. List characteristics of who is doing the bullying.
5. List the characteristics of who is being bullied.

Did You Know?

One in seven children is either someone who bullies or a victim of bullying.

The Three Little Pigs

Do you remember the story of *The Three Little Pigs*?
Each little pig built a house.

Along came the big bad wolf.
He said mean things to the little pigs.
He tried to blow each little pig's house down.

Little pig, little pig, let me come in!

Not by the hair of my chinny, chin, chin. I will not let you in.

1 Finish what the wolf said next.

Then I'll _____ and I'll _____,

And I'll _____ your house _____ !

2 Color the bricks that show how the wolf bullied the pigs.

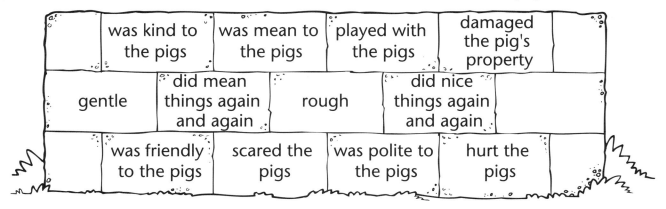

was kind to the pigs	was mean to the pigs	played with the pigs	damaged the pig's property	
gentle	did mean things again and again	rough	did nice things again and again	
was friendly to the pigs	scared the pigs	was polite to the pigs	hurt the pigs	

People can bully, too.

Have you seen someone bully someone else at this school?

On the Playground

Teacher's Notes

Indicator

Participates in a picture story involving a variety of bullying situations.

Teacher Information

Most definitions of bullying agree:
- It is deliberately hurtful, physically or psychologically.
- It is repeated often over time.
- It is difficult for the person being bullied to defend himself/herself against it – he/she is weaker physically or psychologically.

Bullying can be divided into three types:
1. Physical – hitting, punching, pinching, tripping, spitting, kicking, pushing, scratching, damaging, hiding or taking belongings.
2. Verbal – name-calling, making offensive remarks, insulting someone.
3. Emotional – spreading rumors/nasty stories about someone, making fun of someone, excluding from groups, ignoring, ostracizing, alienating.

Discussion Points

(Page 17 can be used as a stand alone picture. Talk with the class along with the discussion points below. Alternatively, students can complete the questions on page 19 after the picture talk, according to their ability levels in reading and writing. Students could also improvise short scenes between two or three children in the picture.)
1. What types of bullying are happening in the picture?
2. Is all name-calling bullying? What names do you get called that you don't mind? When is it bullying?
3. What might the girl watching at the monkey bars be thinking? What can she do?
4. What might the girls sitting on the bench be saying? What might the girl sitting apart be thinking? Why is this bullying? What could she do?
5. Look at the two boys at the edge of the playground punching. Something is wrong, but why might this not be bullying? When would it be bullying?
6. What do you think the boy being called "Fatso" might be thinking?

Did You Know?

The most common form of bullying is verbal.

On the Playground

Teacher's Notes 🕺

Indicator

Views a picture story about bullying situations to answer literal and interpretive comprehension questions.

Students will need to be able to view the picture on page 17 to complete the activity. The activity should be done after the picture talk when most of the questions have been discussed.

Did You Know?

Both boys and girls bully. Usually boys bully boys and girls bully girls.

On the Playground

Look at the picture.
Answer the questions.

1 Put a colored circle around each type of bullying shown in the picture.

> Green – hitting   Orange – name-calling
>
> Red – pushing   Brown – making fun of someone

2 (a) Which type of bullying do you think is the worst?

_____

(b) Why? _____

3 (a) What names do you get called that you don't mind?

_____

(b) Is it bullying if someone calls you one of those names?

4 (a) Write what you think the girls on the bench are saying.

(b) Write what you think the other girl is thinking.

Lunchtime

Teacher's Notes

Indicator

Participates in a picture story involving name-calling as a form of bullying.

Teacher Information

Most definitions of bullying agree:
- It is deliberately hurtful, physically or psychologically.
- It is repeated often over time.
- It is difficult for the person being bullied to defend himself/herself against it – he/she is weaker physically or psychologically.

Bullying can be divided into three types:
1. Physical – hitting, punching, pinching, tripping, spitting, kicking, pushing, scratching, damaging, hiding or taking belongings.
2. Verbal – name-calling, making offensive remarks, insulting someone.
3. Emotional – spreading rumors/nasty stories about someone, making fun of someone, excluding from groups, ignoring, ostracizing, alienating.

Discussion Points

(Page 21 can be used as a stand alone picture. Talk with the class along with the discussion points below. Alternatively, students can complete the questions on page 23 after the picture talk, according to their ability levels in reading and writing. Students could also improvise short scenes between two or three children in the picture.)
1. The same type of bullying is happening in each group. What is it?
2. Is all name-calling bullying? What names do you get called that you don't mind? When is it bullying? (These questions are also discussed on page 16.)
3. What might the girl being called "Freckle Face" be feeling?
   What might the boy being called "Spikey" be feeling?
   What might the boy being called "Slowpoke" be feeling?
4. Discuss what might happen next in each situation in the picture.
5. What do you think the children who have egg or tuna sandwiches will do or say?
6. What could you do if someone teased you or called you names?

Did You Know?

The most common form of verbal bullying is name-calling.

Lunchtime

Lunchtime

Teacher's Notes

Indicator

Views a picture story involving name-calling bullying situations to answer literal and interpretive comprehension questions.

Students will need to be able to see the picture on page 21 to complete the activity. The activity should be done after the picture talk, when most of the questions have been discussed.

Did You Know?

One out of four students is bullied.

Lunchtime

Look at the picture.
Answer the questions.

1 Circle each person who is bullying.

2 No one is touching anyone else in this picture. Why is this still

bullying? _____

_____

_____

3 Write words to show how these two children might be feeling.

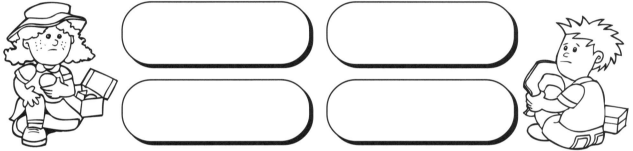

4 Write what you think this boy is thinking.

You're a slowpoke. You eat your lunch slowly and you run slowly. Ha! Ha!

5 What would you do if someone teased you or called you names?

_____

_____

Can I Join in?

Teacher's Notes

Indicator

Participates in a group story involving exclusion from a group as a form of bullying.

Teacher Information

Most definitions of bullying agree:
- It is deliberately hurtful, physically or psychologically.
- It is repeated often over time.
- It is difficult for the person being bullied to defend himself/herself against it – he/she is weaker physically or psychologically.

Bullying can be divided into three types:
1. Physical – hitting, punching, pinching, tripping, spitting, kicking, pushing, scratching, damaging, hiding or taking belongings.
2. Verbal – name-calling, making offensive remarks, insulting someone.
3. Emotional – spreading rumors/nasty stories about someone, making fun of someone, excluding from groups, ignoring, ostracizing, alienating.

Discussion Points

(Page 25 can be used as a stand alone picture. Talk with the class along with the discussion points below. Alternatively, students can complete the questions on page 27 after the picture talk, according to their ability levels in reading and writing. Students could also improvise short scenes between two or three children in the picture.)
1. What type of bullying is happening in the picture?
2. What do you think the girl who is asking to join in might be feeling... before she asked? After she asked?
3. How many children agreed with what was said? What did each of them think?
4. How many children did not agree with what was said? What did each of them think?
5. What do you think will happen next?

Did You Know?

Physical bullying declines with age, but indirect bullying such as exclusion from groups increases.

Can I Join in?

Can I Join in?

Teacher's Notes

Indicator

Views a picture story involving exclusion from a group to answer literal and interpretive comprehension questions.

Students will need to be able to see the picture on page 25 to complete the activity. The activity should be done after the picture talk, when most of the questions have been discussed.

Did You Know?

Boys are more likely to use physical forms of bullying; girls are more likely to use put-downs, spread rumors, practice social exclusion, or use rejection or ostracism.

Can I Join in?

Look at the picture.
Answer the questions.

1 What did the girl ask?

_____

_____

2 What was the answer given by one of the girls?

_____

_____

3 Write words to show how you think the first girl might be feeling.

4 How many children ...

(a) agreed with what she said?

(b) disagreed with what she said?

That was a mean thing to say.

5 What do you think will happen next?

_____

_____

_____

What Is Wrong?

Teacher's Notes

Indicator

Participates in a picture story involving a variety of bullying situations.

Teacher Information

Most definitions of bullying agree:
- It is deliberately hurtful, physically or psychologically.
- It is repeated often over time.
- It is difficult for the person being bullied to defend himself/herself against it – he/she is weaker physically or psychologically.

Bullying can be divided into three types:
1. Physical – hitting, punching, pinching, tripping, spitting, kicking, pushing, scratching, damaging, hiding or taking belongings.
2. Verbal – name-calling, making offensive remarks, insulting someone.
3. Emotional – spreading rumors/nasty stories about someone, making fun of someone, excluding from groups, ignoring, ostracizing, alienating.

Discussion Points

(Page 29 can be used as a stand alone picture. Talk with the class along with the discussion points below. Alternatively, students can complete the questions on page 31 after the picture talk, according to their ability levels in reading and writing. Students could also improvise short scenes between two or three children in the picture.)
1. What is happening in each picture? Is it bullying? How could it be bullying?
2. Why do you think the girl is making up a story about Kate in picture 1? What do you think Kate will do next?
3. Why do you think the children in picture 2 are making faces and giving dirty looks to the girls walking by? What do you think these girls will do next?
4. What do you think the boy in picture 3 will do with Georgia's ruler? The other children are talking to each other and haven't noticed what he is about to do. Do you think he would take it if someone was watching?
5. What do you think will happen next in picture 4? How do you think Blake will feel when he can't find his backpack?
6. What type of bullying do you think is the worst? Why?

Did You Know?

Most bullying takes place in or close to school buildings.

What Is Wrong?

What Is Wrong?

Teacher's Notes 🯅

Indicator

Views a picture story involving a variety of bullying situations to answer literal and interpretive comprehension questions.

Students will need to be able to see the picture on page 29 to complete the activity. The activity should be done after the picture talk, when most of the questions have been discussed.

Did You Know?

In elementary schools the students who bully are often in the same year level as the victim. The victim is usually younger, if there is an age difference.

What Is Wrong?

Look at the picture.
Answer the questions.

1 (a) Circle in red the child in picture 1 who is making up a story.

(b) Why do you think she is doing this?

_____

_____

2 (a) Circle in blue the children in picture 2 who are bullying.

(b) How are they bullying?

_____

_____

3 What do you think the boy in picture 3 will do with Georgia's ruler?

_____

_____

4 What do you think will happen next in picture 4?

_____

_____

_____

5 Which type of bullying do you think is the worst?

Picture (1) (2) (3) (4)

Explain why.

_____

_____

_____

What Do People Who Bully Look Like?

Teacher's Notes 🯄

Indicator

Understands that a person who bullies can be identified by the way he/she acts and not by the way he/she looks.

Teacher Information

Children (or adults) who bully others can come from any kind of family, regardless of social class or cultural background.

People who bully vary in their physical appearance as do the people they bully. It is actions which identify a person who bullies.

Discussion Points

1. Use the pictures on the worksheet and others in magazines to help the students realize that people who bully come in all shapes and sizes. It is important to not use students in the class or school as examples, so as not to—correctly or incorrectly—associate them with bullying.
2. After discussing how people who bully may act, brainstorm with the students and list, "Things a person who bullies may do" and "Things a person who does not bully may do."

Did You Know?

Boys are more likely than girls to engage in bullying behavior (usually physical) and to be the victims of bullies.

What Do People Who Bully Look Like?

Can you tell people who bully by the way they look?
Do you think any of these children would bully others?

You can not tell if someone would bully by the way he/she looks. A person who bullies may be tall or short, big or small, have dark hair or light hair. A person who bullies can be a boy or a girl.
You can only tell a person who bullies by the way he/she acts.

❶ Color the things a person who bullies may do.

hugs you	*takes things belonging to others*	*calls you names*
says mean things	*makes up stories*	*pinches*
punches	*gives dirty looks*	*is polite*	*says nice things*
won't let you join in	*trips you*	*is friendly*

❷ What else might a person who bullies do?

_____

_____

_____

_____

◁ **Why Do People Bully?** ▷

Teacher's Notes

Indicator

- Understands some reasons why people bully.
- Realizes why people may side with a person who bullies.

Teacher Information

People who bully do so for many reasons. They may set out deliberately to bully and feel pleasure in bullying. It may give them a sense of power. A person who bullies may not necessarily lack self-esteem or be insecure; many have average or above-average self-esteem. Their temperaments are more aggressive and they lack empathy. This can be caused by poor parenting and a lack of good role models, or be a personality trait that needs fostering in a positive direction.

A summary of reasons includes:
- They may feel upset or angry or feel they don't fit in.
- They want to seem tough and show off.
- They may get bullied themselves by family members.
- They're scared of getting picked on so do it first.
- If they don't like themselves they may take it out on someone else.
- They think they will become more popular.

Discussion Points

1. Why do you think the boy is saying what he is saying? What if it is true – the other boy can't catch a ball? It is all right to say that?
2. What do you think the friends of the person who is bullying might be thinking? Do they think he is "cool" for having said that? Would it make them like him more? Or less?
3. Why do you think people stay friends with someone who bullies?
4. Should you help someone who is being bullied? How can you help someone who is being picked on?

Did You Know?

Children seem to give positive attention to the bully rather than the victim.

Why Do People Bully?

There are many reasons people might bully others. Sometimes, people who bully think they will look bigger, better, stronger, or be liked more if they bully others.

❶ Why do you think this boy is saying that to the other boy?

_____

_____

❷ Write what you think the friends of the person who is bullying might be thinking.

Sometimes, people pretend to like a person who bullies because they are afraid that person will pick on them as well. It is important to be brave and help someone who is being picked on.

❸ Write one good thing you could do if you saw someone picking on

someone else. _____

_____

_____

How Do People Who Bully Act?

Teacher's Notes

Indicator

Realizes that keeping bullying a secret gives the person bullying more power.

Teacher Information

Students may keep being bullied a secret for a variety of reasons.

These include:
- They think it will get worse and they will suffer more.
- They may appear weak or unable to take care of themselves.
- They do not want to be labeled a tattletale.
- They think teachers can't or won't help them. They may have already told someone, and it was dismissed, so it seems pointless to continue.

Above all, the reason involves fear.

Discussion Points

1. What is a secret? Is it wrong to tell a secret?
2. What things should not be kept a secret? Discuss the pictures in Question 1.
3. Brainstorm and list reasons why someone who is being bullied may keep it a secret.
4. What do you think a person who bullies will do if the bullying stays a secret?
5. Discuss what the person in the picture in Question 3 could do. Students could role-play some of the suggestions.

Did You Know?

Most victims will not tell anyone they are being bullied.

How Do People Who Bully Act?

People who bully know when they are acting in a bad way. They might try to hide their actions from adults to avoid getting into trouble. They might try to make people keep their bullying a secret.

1 Should these things be kept a secret? Discuss each picture.

Yes   No   Yes   No   Yes   No

2 Why might someone who is being bullied not tell anyone?

(i) _____

(ii) _____

(iii) _____

(iv) _____

Keeping bullying a secret will give the person who is bullying more power. He or she will bully again and again.

Every day, Mark tells me he is going to get me at lunchtime. So I never go into the playground. I told the teacher, but Mark said that he didn't say it.

3 What could this person do?

_____

_____

How Do People Who Bully Feel?

Teacher's Notes

Indicator

- Recognizes that people who bully may be hiding how they really feel.
- Suggests ways he/she and the person bullying can prevent the bullying behavior.

Teacher Information

The students bullying in these scenarios are doing so because of a lack of self-esteem (this is not always the case; see page 34).

Did You Know?

Students who bully become less popular as they grow older, until they are eventually disliked by the majority of students.

How Do People Who Bully Feel?

Sometimes people who bully are hiding how they really feel.

1 What could be done to make these people feel better and stop the bullying?

What could they do?	What could you do?

I don't care if I make people feel bad. No one likes me anyway.

If I don't act tough someone might pick on me.

Everyone knows I'm stupid. If I pick on them they will have to listen to me.

If I don't join in with the bullying she might leave me out of the group as well.

Things that Make Me Angry

Teacher's Notes

Indicator

Realizes situations that make them angry and how being angry makes them feel.

Teacher Information

Showing anger does not necessarily mean someone is displaying bullying behavior. It can become this if the behavior is repeated and is physical or verbal to the extreme. Students who bully, however, will more readily adopt aggressive solutions to resolve conflict.

Discussion Points

1. Brainstorm situations where students feel anger and list these on the board.
2. How does being angry make you feel? What do you look like? What do you do? What things are all right to do when you are angry? What things are not all right?
3. Is it okay to be angry sometimes? When?
4. Students can role-play what they have drawn and written about being angry in Question 1 on the worksheet.

Did You Know?

A child's ability to understand emotions is impaired when he/she witnesses adults showing a lot of anger.

Things that Make Me Angry

Some things can make us really angry! Have you ever been really angry?

1 Draw a picture of something which has made you feel angry.
Write what is happening in your picture.

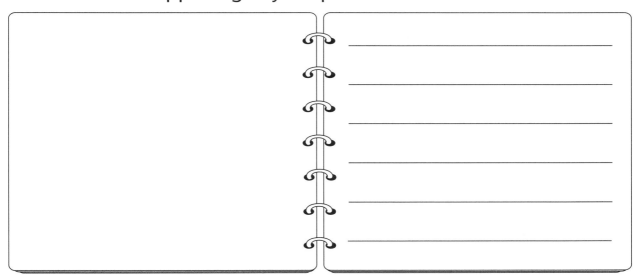

Sometimes, when people are angry they do bad things. Later, they might wish they had not done them.

Doing bad things when you are angry is never okay.

2 Color the words describing how being angry made you feel.

3 Put a red cross on the boxes that are things we might feel – but must not do.

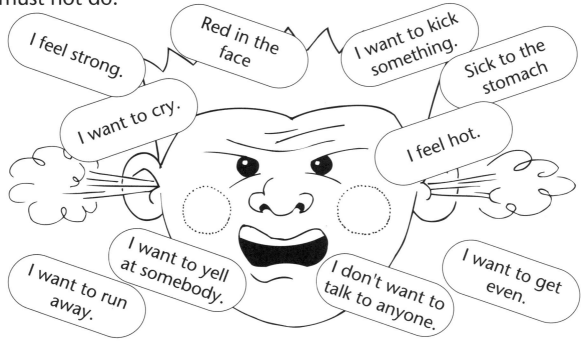

What Should I Do if I Am Angry?

Teacher's Notes

Indicator

Identifies ways to deal with feeling angry.

Teacher Information

As a teacher, you can help children deal with anger in a socially acceptable way. Unacceptable ways of expressing anger include hitting and pushing, sulking and crying excessively, or constantly looking for comfort solutions from a teacher or adult.

Encouraging students to follow the steps on the worksheet will help them deal with anger. Talking about how they feel and developing an empathy towards others will help them to gain control of their emotions.

Teachers can assist by listening to students and suggesting to them how to act and feel in different situations where they experience anger.

Discussion Points

1. Is it all right to be angry? What things shouldn't you do when you are angry? What do you do when you are angry?
2. Is it all right to hurt someone or his/her feelings when you are angry?
3. What could you do if you feel yourself becoming angry?
4. Role-play a situation where anger is building up and use the steps listed on the worksheet to control their emotions.

Did You Know?

A child's ability to understand emotions is impaired when he/she witnesses adults showing a lot of anger.

What Should I Do if I Am Angry?

Doing bad things when you are angry is not okay!

Different people act in different ways when they are angry. Often, people who bully use being angry as an excuse for doing bad things to other people.

If you get angry, you have a choice about how to act. Being angry doesn't make you do bad things!

If you get angry you need to:

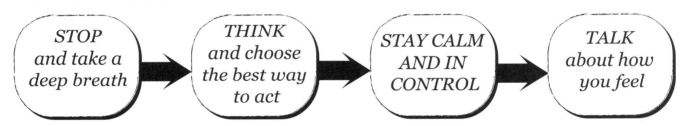

STOP and take a deep breath → THINK and choose the best way to act → STAY CALM AND IN CONTROL → TALK about how you feel

❶ What do you do when you feel angry? _____

_____

❷ Does the way you act when you are angry hurt other people or their feelings?  Yes No

❸ Do you need to change the way you act when you are angry?  Yes No

❹ If you feel yourself becoming angry, what could you do?

_____

_____

_____

Everyone Should Feel Safe

Teacher's Notes

Indicator

Understands that bullying can cause someone to be hurt and everyone has a right to feel safe.

Teacher Information

Physical bullying such as pushing, hitting, tripping, pinching, or spitting can cause someone to get hurt. It may be unintentional, but the possible consequences should be discussed with students.

Discussion Points

1. What is happening in the picture? What do you think could happen next?
2. Is it wrong to push someone? Is it bullying? When can it be bullying?
3. What should happen to the boy pushing in the picture?
4. Has something like this happened to you?

Did You Know?

Physical bullying declines with age, but indirect bullying such as exclusion from groups increases.

Everyone Should Feel Safe

Everyone has the right to feel safe.

1 (a) What is happening in this picture?_____

_____

(b) What do you think could happen next?

_____

_____

_____

_____

_____

(c) What do you think should happen to the person pushing?

_____

_____

Bullying can include pushing, hitting, spitting, tripping, or pinching.

2 Draw and write about a type of bullying you have seen or which has happened to you.

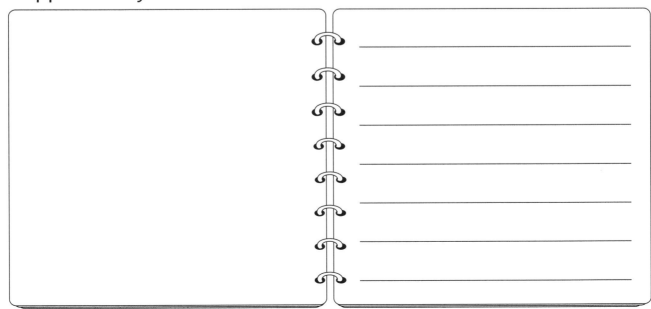

The Sandbox

Teacher's Notes

Indicator

- Sequences a set of pictures involving a bullying situation in the sandbox.
- Suggests how he/she could deal with this situation.

Discussion Points

1. Discuss what is happening in each picture and the correct order to cut out and sequence.
2. What do you think could happen next? (The boy could throw the sand and hurt the others if it gets in their eyes; the two boys may give up the dump truck and the person bullying will have "won;" the two boys may persuade the other to wait his turn; the two boys may tell the teacher, etc.)
3. Students could role-play this situation in groups of three and use the different solutions suggested as endings.

Did You Know?

Four times out of every five, an argument with someone who bullies will wind up as a physical fight.

The Sandbox

Look at the pictures below.

Color the pictures, then cut them out and glue in the correct order.

In the blank box, draw how you would deal with this situation.

Bullying Can Make You Worry

Teacher's Notes

Indicator

Understands how bullying can affect a person's health and/or his/her ability to learn.

Teacher Information

One group of children who are victims of bullying often lack self-esteem, are oversensitive, feel insecure and are not as big or strong as the person who is bullying. The latter has a physical, and more importantly, a psychological power. The victims usually behave passively or submissively and do not retaliate when bullied.

Other victims provoke tension and annoy others with their active, irritating behavior. When bullied, they will retaliate.

Constant bullying can result in short and long-term consequences. These include:
• The stress and feeling of depression may lead to stomach aches or headaches, excessive weeping or crying, bed-wetting, nightmares or sleeping difficulties.
• Self-esteem drops, along with the students' self-image.
• Victims may be reluctant to attend school.

It is important to address bullying early, as it becomes difficult to break the cycle later, either for the victim or the bully.

Discussion Points

1. When you are worried about something, how does it make you feel?
2. Have you ever been worried about being bullied by someone?
3. What could you do if you are worried about being bullied?

Did You Know?

8% of students miss one day of school a month to avoid being bullied.

Bullying Can Make You Worry

When someone keeps bullying you all the time it can make you feel very upset. You start to worry more and more. What can worry do?

- It can make you feel **sick**.
- It can give you a **tummy ache**.
- If can give you a **headache**.
- It can make you **cry**.

1 What else can worry do?_____

_____

2 Use the words in bold print to label what can happen to someone who is worrying about a bully.

It can make you
_____.

(Draw the tears.)

It can give you a
_____.

(Color where it aches.)

It can give you a
_____.

(Color where it aches.)

You can feel
_____.

(Color where you feel this.)

3 What happens to you when you feel worried?

_____

_____

When you are worried it makes it hard to listen and learn at school. **Everyone has the right to learn and not be worried.**

4 What can you do if you are worried about being bullied?

_____

_____

How Do You Feel?

Teacher's Notes

Indicator

Matches facial expressions depicting feelings to pictures showing bullying situations.

Teacher Information

Students will choose different faces representing the emotions felt in each situation according to how much they are bullied or inclined to bully.

Discussion Points

1. Brainstorm types of feelings with the students and draw a face depicting each emotion on the board. List situations when students feel each emotion. Some may cover more than one – e.g., birthday party (happy, excited).
2. What is happening in each picture on the worksheet? What do you think each person who is being bullied feels? How would you feel?
3. What could you do if you were the person being bullied? What could you do if you were the person who saw these things happening?

Did You Know?

There are three ways of responding to bullying: being passive, aggressive, or assertive. Generally, people who bully tend to be aggressive while their victims tend to be passive.

How Do You Feel?

1 Look at the pictures. Color the face which shows how you would feel if this was happening to you.

Problems I Can Solve

Teacher's Notes

Indicator

Uses problem-solving strategies through discussion and role-playing.

Teacher Information

Teaching problem-solving strategies through discussion and role-playing will assist students in learning and developing skills for positive social behaviors and relationships.

Discussion Points

1. Do you always agree with what someone says or does? Should everyone agree with you? Should you agree with everyone?
2. If you have a problem, what do you do? Are you a fair problem-solver? Are you good at solving problems?
3. (Discuss the problem-solving rules worksheet.) How would you solve the problem shown in the picture? (Discuss ideas and role-play suggestions by students.)

Did You Know?

On average, bullying episodes are usually very short, lasting for about 37 seconds.

Problems I Can Solve

Everyone is different. We do things in different ways and we often want different things. Sometimes we don't agree with other people and there can be a problem.

1 Read the "Problem-solving Rules" and discuss how this problem could be solved.

Can I play in your game?

No! We don't want you to play.

Problem-solving Rules

- *Try to solve problems so that* **everyone wins***.*

- **Let people know** *how you feel.*

- **Listen** *to how other people feel.*

- **Say sorry** *if you hurt someone's feelings.*

- **Be fair** *to everyone.*

2 Fill in the speech balloons to show how they could solve their problem.

3 Are you a fair problem solver?   (Yes)   (No)

What Can I Do if I Am Bullied?

Teacher's Notes

Indicator

Matches suggestions to a picture scenario about what to do if he/she is bullied.

Teacher Information

It is imperative students realize that bullying is not to be tolerated and they should not put up with it if it is happening to them.

The worksheet shows students some suggestions to tackle bullying.

These are some things the students should *not* do.
1. Try to keep dealing with the problem themselves – it is all right to ask for help.
2. Exaggerate or not tell the true facts. If a part of what they say is shown to be untrue, it casts doubt upon the whole situation.
3. Don't retaliate by hitting, etc. They could end up being accused of bullying themselves.

Discussion Points

1. Discuss how everyone has the right to feel safe and does not deserve to be bullied.
2. What should you do if you are bullied? (Brainstorm suggestions.) What might happen if you don't do something about it? (Discuss with students that people who are bullying keep doing so until they are stopped.)
3. The first three pictures on the worksheet show things students can do to try to stop being bullied. These things could be tried before getting help if the bullying is not too severe. Each is an example of assertive behavior, yet calm and rational. Discuss with the students.
4. In picture 4, the student is asking an adult for help. Ask the students the special people they know who they could ask for help. (Teacher, parent, older friend, etc.) Students could draw and label pictures of people they trust.

Did You Know?

Many adults do not know how to intervene in bullying situations; therefore, bullying is overlooked.

What Can I Do if I Am Bullied?

No one deserves to be bullied!
No one has the right to hurt anyone!
If you are being bullied you need to DO SOMETHING about it.
People who bully keep doing so until they are stopped.
Here are some good things to do if someone is bullying you.

1 Cut the labels and glue them to the matching picture.

Go to a safe place.
Stay around other people.

Tell the person who is bullying that you don't like it.

Don't tease or hit back.
Look strong and walk away.

Go to an adult you trust. Tell him/her the truth about what is happening.

Telling the Teacher

Teacher's Notes

Indicator

- Understands the reasons why someone may not want to tell about bullying.
- Understands the importance of telling the truth.

Teacher Information

Students may be reluctant to inform a teacher about bullying because:
- They do not want to be labeled as tattletales.
- They think it will make it worse.
- They feel that teachers can't or won't be able to help them.

Students must realize bullying is not to be tolerated and that the only way to stop bullying is to be open about it with actions or words. Keeping it a secret from adults they trust gives the bullies more power to continue. That is why they go to so much trouble to try to stop victims from telling.

Students should also realize the importance of telling the truth. If a part of what they say is untrue then it casts doubt on the situation. They must also differentiate between a friendly tease as opposed to an intentionally upsetting remark that continues.

Discussion Points

1. Why is it hard for a teacher to know who is telling the truth? Why is it important to always tell the truth?
2. Has someone told a tale about you? How did you feel?
3. When should you tell the teacher about something that happened to you?
4. Why might someone be afraid to tell the teacher he/she is being bullied?
5. Why do people who bully want to keep it a secret?

Did You Know?

Over 70% of teachers say they always intervene in a bullying situation but only 25% of students agree with them!

Telling the Teacher

Some people who bully tell the teacher stories they have made up to get other people into trouble.

It can be hard for the teacher to know who is telling the truth!

1 Has someone ever told the teacher a story about you?

I am being bullied – but I don't want to tell the teacher.

2 How did it make you feel?

_____

3 Write three reasons why Alice might not want to tell the teacher she is being bullied.

(i) _____

_____

(ii) _____

_____

(iii) _____

If you are being bullied, you don't have to deal with it on your own – ask the teacher for help!

People who bully might try to make you keep the way they treat you a secret.

Tell the teacher the truth!

Don't keep bullying a secret!

You'd better not tell the teacher – or else!

4 Why would someone who is bullying not want you to tell the teacher what he/she has done?

_____

_____

5 Why is it important to tell the teacher the truth?

_____

Helping Others

Teacher's Notes

Indicator

- Gives reasons why some people take the side of someone bullying.
- Understands his/her responsibilities if he/she witnesses a bullying incident.

Teacher Information

Students who witness bullying may act in the following ways:
- Help the person bullying by joining in.
- Help the person bullying by watching, laughing, or shouting encouragement.
- Remain completely uninvolved.
- Help the person being bullied by telling the person bullying to stop or getting an adult, etc.

Bullying usually happens where the person doing the bullying has an "audience" of other children. It might be people they don't know or a group of their friends. If an adult is nearby, though, such as a teacher, bullies can be very careful about not letting the adult see what they are doing.

When a group of people bully, there is often a "leader" and "followers" who go along with what the leader is doing or saying. Sometimes the followers do not really agree with what the leader is doing, but might feel that they have to. This is sometimes called "peer pressure."

Openly discussing ways for students to assist others who are being bullied will help foster an anti-bullying attitude in the school.

Discussion Points

1. What is happening in the picture?
2. Why do you think the others are agreeing with the person bullying? Is this bullying itself?
3. Two students are laughing with the person bullying, but don't really agree with what he is doing. Why do you think this is?
4. Should Chad be helped? Why?
   How could you help Chad in this situation?
5. Brainstorm the ways they can help students who are being bullied in their school.

Did You Know?

Playground statistics have shown that – every seven minutes a child is bullied – adult intervention 4% – peer intervention 11% – no intervention 85%.

Helping Others

Look at the picture and answer the questions below.

1 Explain what is happening in this picture. _____

_____

2 Why do you think the others are encouraging the fight?_____

_____

3 Are the others bullying? ⬭Yes⬭ ⬭No⬭

4 How could you stay safe and still help Chad? _____

_____

If you know someone is being bullied – do something about it!

5 Color the T-shirts that say the things **you** are going to do to help the people being bullied in your school.

We Are All Different

Teacher's Notes

Indicator

Realizes that no one is exactly the same and everyone has a right to be valued.

Teacher Information

Students have the right to be valued for their individuality, including race, gender, culture and physical and intellectual differences. Tolerance of others is the key focus in this lesson.

Discussion Points

1. Make headings on the board according to the worksheet. Collate and tally lists under each heading. Focus on the variety of answers for students to realize the differences in their own class.

Did You Know?

Victims of bullying are more likely to tell parents than teachers.

We Are All Different

People are many DIFFERENT shapes and sizes.

They have DIFFERENT colored hair, eyes and skin.

People like to do DIFFERENT things.

No one is exactly the same.

1 Choose a partner in your class you do not usually talk to or play with. Find out more about each other by filling in the lists.

Draw a picture.

Me: _____   My Friend: _____

	hair color	
	eye color	
	skin color	
	likes to eat	
	likes to do	
	likes to watch on television	
	interesting facts about this person	

Nobody has the right to bully somebody else because he or she looks different or likes to do different things.

Talking and Listening

Teacher's Notes

Indicator

Understands there is a time to talk and a time to listen.

Teacher Information

The Native American "talking stick" can be used to teach and practice tolerance in listening and communicating. In many tribes, the "talking stick" was used to ensure each person had a turn to share his/her thoughts, feelings, ideas and opinions. Only the person with the stick was allowed to speak. While this person spoke, everyone else was expected to listen respectfully.

If using this in class, don't insist that a student has to speak unless he/she wants to. Shyer students may take longer to gain enough confidence.

Before dealing with sensitive issues, wait until all students feel safe and confident about speaking in the circle.

Discussion Points

1. Some people are good at talking, others are good at listening, and some are good at both. Ask students what they think about themselves.
2. What would happen if everyone wanted to speak at once?
3. Do you think the "talking stick" is a good idea?
4. Do you think there is a time to talk and a time to listen?

Did You Know?

Children involved in bullying (whether bullying or being bullied) usually have poor social skills and problems at home.

Talking and Listening

1 What would happen if everyone in the class wanted to talk at the same time?

_____

_____

There is a time to **talk** to others and a time to **listen** to others.

2 What do you do in your class if you would like to speak?

_____

_____

Did you know that in Native American tribes, people used a "talking stick"? Only the person with the stick was allowed to speak. That way each person had a turn to say something while the others listened. When the person finished speaking, he or she passed the stick onto someone else.

Your class could try using a "talking stick." It could be a ruler or just a thick stick.

3 Write something you would like to say with the stick. Your teacher will tell you the topic.

Topic: _____

Making Rules

Teacher's Notes

Indicator

Understands the importance of setting rules to help avoid conflict and when and how to set them.

Teacher Information

Working out clear rules before a game begins and making the rules as fair as possible for everyone helps prevent potential conflicts before they arise.

Changing the rules to suit him/herself is one way a person who bullies may behave towards victims.

Discussion Points

1. Why are rules important? What could happen if there were no rules?
2. What kind of things do we make rules for? Brainstorm a list.
3. When would be the best time to make up rules for a game?
4. Has somebody ever changed the rules during a game you were playing? If so, how did you feel? Why do you think that person changed the rules? Is it fair?
5. What do you think will happen next in the picture? Students could role-play this situation and possible outcomes.

Did You Know?

Unless new behaviors are adopted, students who bully will continue to do so. By 24, up to 60% of children who bully will have at least one criminal conviction.

Making Rules

Rules are made so everyone can be happy, healthy and safe in what they are doing.

Rules can be made for the classroom, the playground, at home, when playing games and for the road.

1 What could happen if there were no rules?

_____

_____

2 Pretend you are going to play tag with some friends. When would be the best time to make rules?

| before the game | in the middle of the game | at the end of the game |

3 How would you feel if someone kept trying to change the rules?

happy ☐   worried ☐   sad ☐   angry ☐   scared ☐

4 Ryan was out in the baseball game. Write what you think each person is thinking.

I'm NOT out!

Remember: Rules should be fair for everyone.
Everyone should stick to the rules.

Sharing and Taking Turns

Teacher's Notes

Indicator

Understands that cooperating by sharing and taking turns will help avoid conflict.

Teacher Information

Focusing on students cooperating through sharing and taking turns teaches them how we should treat others and be treated in turn.

Not waiting his/her turn and not sharing are ways a person who bullies may behave towards victims.

Discussion Points

1. How can we care for other people? Brainstorm a list of suggestions.
2. How do you care for others at school?
3. How are the children in the pictures caring about each other? What do you think the children in the pictures might be saying?
4. How are the children in the pictures cooperating?

Students could role-play these situations in pairs or small groups.

Did You Know?

Body language is an important part of communication. Psychologists say the impact we have on others depends on **what** we say (7%), **how** we say it (38%) and our **body** (nonverbal) language (55%).

Sharing and Taking Turns

Caring people share things with other people.

1 Write words in the speech balloons to show these children sharing.

When people share they COOPERATE.

Caring people take turns and remember to give other people a turn.

2 Write words in the speech balloons to show these children taking turns.

When people take turns they COOPERATE.

3 What does COOPERATE mean?

_____

_____

4 Are you good at cooperating?

Being a Good Friend

Teacher's Notes

Indicator

Understands how to make a student new to the school feel happy and safe.

Teacher Information

When a student is new to a school it can be hard to make new friends and find a group to fit in with. Some students may play on a new student's insecurity and pick on or even bully him/her.

Encouraging and discussing ways students could interact with new students helps create a positive, welcoming atmosphere, with students being more open and understanding of how newcomers may be feeling.

Discussion Points

1. Have you ever moved to a new house or school? How did you feel? (or) How do you think you would feel?
2. How do you think Harry is feeling about going to his new school?
3. How could you make Harry feel welcome?

Students could role-play in pairs.

Did You Know?

Children of bullies often become bullies themselves and will probably continue to bully as adults unless they get help.

Being a Good Friend

"Hi! My name is Harry. I have just moved to a new house and had to leave all my friends behind at my last school. It's a bit scary being the new kid."

1 Write or draw three things you could do to make Harry feel welcome.

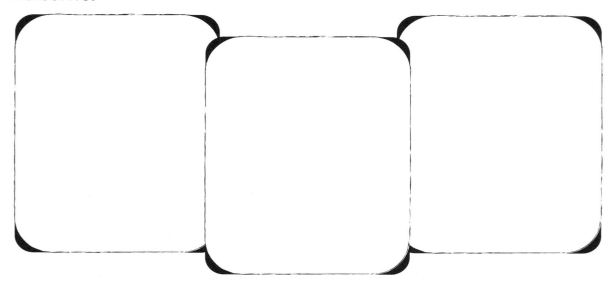

2 Color the children who would make Harry feel happy and safe at school.

I would show him around the school.

I would not share my pencils with him.

I would not let him play in our game.

I would eat my lunch with him.

I would play with him.

Acts of Kindness

Teacher's Notes

Indicator

Understands the reciprocal feelings of doing an act of kindness and having it done to him/her.

Teacher Information

Thinking of and doing acts of kindness helps promote a positive, caring atmosphere in the school. Negative acts such as bullying will be less tolerated as "acts of kindness" become second nature.

Discussion Points

1. What does it feel like to be kind? To be mean?
   How does it feel when someone is kind to you? Mean to you?
2. How can you be kind to others? Brainstorm a list.
3. How is each person being kind in the pictures?

Students could role-play these and other situations showing acts of kindness.

Did You Know?

When people who are bullies in elementary school grow up, they will need more government support, have more court convictions, be more likely to be alcoholics, will be more antisocial and need more mental health care.

Acts of Kindness

Other people will care about you if you care about them. Here are some ways you can show you care about another person.

1 Match each way of showing you care to a picture.

| using manners | listening to others | including others | cooperating with others | being fair |

We all like to feel special!

It is easy to do nice things for other people and it makes them feel very special!

2 Think of someone in your class you don't talk to very often.

Write his/her name in the box.

What could you do and say to make him/her feel special?

Do...

Say...

Try it out! Did you make your person feel special?

Notes